THE LOGISTICS ADVANTAGE

Common Sense, Logistics, & Transportation

Hugo Soto

To my Family

FOREWORD

Whether you're a business entrepreneur or a college student, you are probably are looking at this book because you want to understand and successfully manage transportation logistics. Because this is a fast-moving, dynamic area of expertise, I've designed this book to help you hit the ground running by sharing my own experience, education, and ideologies. This book is a functional guide, not a textbook. There will be no quizzes, vocabulary sections, or tests at the end. My goal is to share some important points for consideration and provide some memorable anecdotes that will help you address issues in the field. I begin with philosophy and theory, then drill down to practical daily knowledge.

When I graduated from the University of Houston, I was optimistic and naïve. I had studied hard and passed my supply chain courses with flying colors, but when I started working in logistics, one thing became painfully clear. The road from college theory classes to real-life practice is obstructed by smart, experienced field workers, laughing at and telling stories at the bar about at cocky, young, college-educated professionals who are convinced they know more.

ABOUT THE AUTHOR

All my life I dreamed of growing up and wearing a suit and tie to work. Seriously. In my dreams, I'd wear Hugo Boss: shined oxfords; dark slim-fit business shirt and two-piece suit; silk tie and pocket handkerchief; gold cufflinks; and signature fragrance. When I walked in to my office, people noticed. I was envied and admired for my intelligence, looks, and lifestyle. Think "Suits," but Harvey the lawyer is Hugo the business executive. I dedicated myself to the study of business, and or a while I fed the fantasy by wearing polished shoes, a suit, and occasional tie as practice for the real world.

By the time I entered the "real world," however, I realized fashion does not guarantee success in logistics. In fact, my dress office attire is a button-down shirt (usually with the sleeves rolled up) and slacks, with a tie only for special meetings or events. Casual Fridays are for nice jeans with polo shirts, and working from home usually entails pajamas.

You might wonder how I let go of my suit-wearing dreams and replaced it with a career I am truly passionate about. Sometime about halfway through my college education, I realized how much I enjoyed going to my supply chain classes. They were the classes that inherently made sense to me, while some of my peers struggled with the concepts. To me, supply chain theory was not that different from the efficiency, common sense, and organizational practices I strive for in my daily life.

I recognized that the precepts I'd established for my finances, relationships, physical and mental growth, basically my life, would be the tools that ensure my professional success.

Degree

I graduated with a degree in Supply Chain with specializations in Energy Supply Management and Strategic Sourcing from the University of Houston. I worked two jobs to get through college. I must admit it took me a bit longer than most, but I graduated with no debt. I also joined a fraternity and enjoyed all the social, academic, and professional benefits that come from such organizations.

Jobs I've held

I've worked many different jobs that have provided me unique experiences. I've been a shop keeper for a small grocery in Mexico, sold pecans I gathered from my grandfather's farm at the local Market, and worked for a novelty store as a cashier. I worked for a successful event caterer and did street marketing for a large tech company. I was also employed as an analyst for another tech company. I've taught computer classes as a public service and worked as an underwriter for a small financial company. I worked as a business process manager before becoming an oil and gas contract analyst. From there I transitioned to a North American logistics planner for a large energy corporation.

NON-LOGISTICIANS VS. LOGISTICIANS

In my opinion there are will always be people who are born with certain qualities necessary to excel in certain arenas. Some are natural athletes; others may have inherent talent for art, music, math or science. I see logistics specialists no differently. There are some people who are naturally suited for this job, but ultimately, I believe anyone can become a successful logistician who has the desire to improve and willingness to learn. Hustle always eventually trumps talent.

Personalities

We all have that one friend who seems to have it all together. Perhaps they manage time exceptionally well, no matter the circumstances that intervene. They are mysteriously unaffected by traffic, illness, or relationship calamities. They will always be the person who arrives first and ends up holding the seats for their more human friends. Perhaps it's the kind of friend that is always prepared. He has an umbrella handy when storms suddenly break out on a sunny day; he has complete notes with him for the entire semester; there is a first aid kit in the glove compartment of their immaculate and fully equipped car. Or it might be the friend who can plan a perfect party, with no detail unaccounted for from venue to decorations to music to lighting to designated drivers for those who drink one too many.

The pinball wizard with perfect timing, the boy scout who is always prepared, and the detail diva who can sync any event are a few examples of personalities that can thrive in logistics., If none of these sound like you, don't worry. After reading this book, and with a little real-life practice, you might find yourself becoming one of those awe-inspiring who have it all together.

Learned Skills and Traits

Chances are the people you think have it all together learned their tricks the same way I did: from experience, advice, and role models. It may be that the friend throwing those spectacular parties grew up with a parent who was an event planner. The person who is always on time may have had a pizza delivery job growing up. Equally likely, the friend who is always prepared may be an Eagle Scout. Your experiences are uniquely yours and may not have introduced you to the skills or mindset needed for logistics. The important thing is that you can continue learning all your life, if you wish to do so. Whether or not you capitalize on that is your choice.

New Perspective

I love the phrase "To a man with a hammer, everything looks like a nail" for several reasons. First, because I enjoy people whose solution to every technological malfunction is to start banging at it. Even funnier when it works. Secondly, it implies that people with only one skill set will use it to fix every problem they come across. Some jobs may require multiple tools and skills, but logistics is a very useful tool for fixing almost any problem

You might hesitate to use logistics to fix a broken computer, but you might use it to make a decision between buying a new one or using one at your school. You might use logistics to determine the fastest, safest route to the store with the best deal on that computer. Amazon will use logistics to get a new one to you, if you decide you want one delivered. Amazon has an entire logistics department dedicated to moving freight from their suppliers, to their warehouses, to your doorstep. Perhaps, if you're good at logistics, companies like Amazon will hire you and pay you enough money to purchase a new computer every time yours breaks.

To Make It Easy

Plain and simple, the main goal of this book is to make your life easier, when dealing with the day to day challenges of home and work. Reading this book may help you save money while trying to determine the best way to supply your products to clients. If you're considering a career in logistics, it may help you make sense of your career choice within the field.

To Make It Safe

One of the biggest challenges with managing logistics is safety. Safety for yourself, your bottom line, your business, your neighborhood, and, potentially, your country. That isn't much of an exaggeration considering our world is continuously evolving into a global marketplace. That type of market requires moving materials from different countries to different countries, designing a plan and implementing a system to get products to recipient countries for distribution and use. Whether you're a student, employee, or business owner being aware of all the intricate details is to your ultimate advantage.

To Help You Out

At the end of the day, I want for you the same things I want for myself. A brighter future. With a flourishing business and a growing bank account, by which you could afford the best college education for your children. I want you to move on up the corporate ladder to the positions that come with corner offices and exquisite window views. I want you to be mortgage free, take amazing vacations, and be able to buy all those unnecessary luxuries that just make your soul feel good. If I can make your life just a little easier each day, that alone may go a long way towards helping you determine your best life.

THE LOGISTICS MINDSET

The idea behind creating a logistics mindset is simple. If you want to be a logistician, you must think like one. Somewhat cliché statements such as "think like a man," "you need to think like a criminal to catch a criminal," and "it takes one to know one" make a valid point. I won't try to sell you on adapting a logistics mindset to rule your entire life but let me highlight the benefits. I'm an advocate of changing your mindset to emulate the activities that you're passionate about. When I write, I think like a writer, when I paint, I think like a painter, when I'm at work, I think like a logistician. When you need to be a logistician, think like a logistician and reap the benefits of efficiency, flexibility, and logic.

The Sight of the Oracle

The first seemingly magical skill set of a good logistician is their uncanny ability to predict the future. Besides a reason-based sense of how future events will unfold, a good logistician must be able to adapt and change it. That is a skill I call the "Sight of the Oracle," or simply "the sight". I'll spend some time helping you develop it for yourself but first I want to advise you of some crucial aspects of logistics that most people would love to ignore.

The first step to developing the sight is simply to read. Read everything. Fiction, non-fiction, biographies, thrillers, romances, how-to guides, political, classics, business, psychology, anything and everything you can. This will provide you a good foundation of possibilities within a wide range of scenarios. The more you read, the more possibilities you'll become aware of, and that will help you predict how things turn out. Watching television does not allow you to absorb the full effects of all the possibilities the way the written word does because you aren't actively engaging your imagination. Which leads me to my next point.

The second practice is to use your imagination. You can do this very simply, as in this transportation example: You are responsible for scheduling a shipment of fruit from a Texas farm to a New York store. Close your eyes, and imagine the entire travel of your shipment, from where its current location to its destination. Picture the roads it will travel, how it will be stored, packaged, move, the shipping needs, and any other related details. Now, do that exercise as many times in as many different scenarios necessary to make the best decisions. When you initially imagine the transportation, you realize possibility of rotting fruit, you improve modify your scenario by arranging for refrigerated transport. Next imagine your package was delayed. Now you modify your decision again, searching for ways to move it faster and more efficiently. During that process, you realize the boxes could allow bruising or other damage to the product, so you begin thinking of better packaging ideas. The decisions made in each scenario improve your prediction by anticipating possible problems and refining your initial plan. I know it is unrealistic to expect anyone could foresee ALL the problems that might come up, but that's not the point. You are simply using this exercise to minimize the margin of error in your predicted transportation scenario.

One final point about the logistics mindset: Learn from mistakes, particularly the past mistakes of others. Every logistics specialist knows two things

    1. The unexpected always happens. Keep calm and remember Murphy's Law (Anything that can go wrong, will go wrong.

    2. Most logistical knowledge is gleaned from experience.

Understand there will be mistakes and associated costs. Those are sunk costs that we need to prepare for and will continue to present themselves unless we learn from experience. You can't view mistakes as isolated incidents that will only happen once, and so you shouldn't chew out your employees for making mistakes. The only thing to do is bite the bullet on the costs of mistakes, then learn from them so they become less and less impactful in the future. In this field, what you don't know CAN hurt you, and oftentimes you don't know, what you don't know.

The Benefits of Negativity

Pessimists are great logisticians since they are so adept at predicting what is going to go wrong. These are the people who can anticipate the worst-case scenario in everything and have made an art form of expecting the unexpected. They are the people who will prevent you from making the most mistakes. The world tends to frown upon pessimists, dismiss them, and ignore their warnings. This itself is a big mistake. In my experience, when things go badly, the pessimist will be the one with the "I told you so" look on his face; he probably did tell you 70% of the time. The other 30% he knew the possibilities but remained silent.

I am not suggesting you take the sunshine out of your life and install a permanent raincloud over your head, but if you have a team, or the opportunity to put one together, I'm advising you to always make sure you have a pessimist. If you don't, the next best thing is asking advice from a pessimist that understands the problem.

The Benefits of Positivity

Optimists are also great at logistics, but for vastly different reasons. Optimists are great problem solvers because they can visualize possibilities. When faced with a problem, they see solutions other people can't. When the world is out of answers, they are the people that see opportunity instead of a world full of challenges and problems.

I'm not advocating for blind optimism either, but I want to recognize the important role optimism plays in logistics. The optimist are the problem solvers that will tell you how it can work or give you the ideas that will bring home the money. Rule of thumb always have an optimist on your team, especially when you're in a tough spot or out of ideas.

Finding the Most Likely Scenarios

The realist is the optimal logistics machine. Unfortunately, people only call themselves realists after being accused pessimism. It is impossible to be entirely unbiased and always have all the necessary facts. As Logisticians need to make logical decisions with as much information as possible. We need to know all the resources at our disposal, the products we are moving, road restrictions (both physical and legal), and we need to have realistic plans and expectations to excel at our chosen craft.

The path to realism begins with a few axioms that will tie down your reality. Create a few unshakeable beliefs to secure all other. I can't tell you what they should all be. They will vary by person, industry, and situation; but I can give you a few guidelines that will get you thinking along the right path. I try to avoid from clichés as much as possible, but many of them make good axioms.

1. Murphy's Law, everything that can go wrong, will go wrong, so be aware and ready.

2. What you don't know, can hurt you. Spend time daily bettering yourself, reading, running through scenarios, perfecting your processes, etc.

3. Everybody sees the world differently, the word "fast" to you might mean something different to your employees, to your coworkers, to your teammates, to your customers. Always be as specific and clear as possible.

If you learn nothing else from this book, those three axioms alone, will make you a better logistician. As we go on, I'll get more technical and practical, so hopefully you will be able to draw on axioms more particular to your situation.

THE GOAL MAKES THE LOGISTICIAN

There are multiple types of logisticians, depending on the industry, field, expertise, etc. There is no good way to consolidate them and teach specific information for all of them in one book. A logistician in a medical field will always be different from a military logistician, who will always be different than a corporate logistician. Given that a lot of the skills are transferable, however, I hope this book will be helpful to each type in one way or another. To help with that, I have categorized the different types of logisticians by end goal.

The Results Logistician

The first type of logistician is quite simply the guy who must get it done. The logistician whose boss says, "I don't care how you do it, just get it done." This type of logistician faces the constraints of uncommon situations, tight deadlines, and flexible methodologies. Usually money is an afterthought, the resources needed vary widely depending on the situation, and creativity is an essential skillset.

The most important skill for this type of logistician is wits. If in your current life, this is the type of logistician you need to be, spend a lot of time reading (both books and articles), keep up with technology, and practice creative hobbies that will sharpen your wits and make you better suited for those logistics requirements (writing, painting, building things etc.) .

The Optimizing Logistician

This type of logistician is concerned with one thing, optimizing profits. The logistician whose boss says, "I want you to spend the absolute minimum possible and still get the job done." This logistician, whether at a small business or a large corporation, is responsible for moving things from one place to another at the lowest cost. With all the responsibility this position brings, it is important to operate between the lines of saving money and making sure the jobs still gets done.

The most important skill set for this type of logistician, is data management. Tracking, analyzing, and understanding the data are crucial tools for cost management and ensuring the work continues being done. This logistician should spend some time sharpening their tech skills, learning to use Excel, working on puzzles, and reading a few business books about data handling, time management, and successful business practices of world class companies.

The Emergency Logistician

The third category is the emergency logistician. Usually this person gets called when everything has already gone wrong, the expert people call to get everyone else out of trouble. This logistician may get books and movies written about them, but mistakes can be career ending. This is also the category that all logisticians will eventually get thrown into and often must handle without much help.

Whether you're regularly the guy saving everyone's bacon or life has thrown you into a sink or swim situation, the emergency logistician needs to have resources. I don't necessarily mean money, although that's always a great resource to have, but knowing exactly who to call for help in any situation. Having tools and specialized skill sets or knowing people who have those skill sets will get you out of trouble. The emergency logistician needs to understand the available technology and use it to solve problems in ways that haven't been seen before. For this logistician it is important to network regularly, keep up to date with technology, and keep a few aces up their sleeves.

The Master Logistician

The master logistician is a title I would reserve only for those who have mastered the previous three types of logistician categories. The ultimate goal is to be capable of handling every imaginable situation, using logistical superpowers to come up with creative solutions,; manipulate data to test, track, and back up their decisions; and have the resources to make changes and prevent high-stress situations on a grand scale.

The master logistician is the person who has dedicated his professional career to mastering the art of logistics in their field and can handle any situation that presents itself. To be this kind of logistician, you must actively practice all the recommendations previously mentioned and continuously test your skills in your respective field.

Things Happen

As in life, the one certainty in logistics is things will go wrong. Things happen, plain and simple, and someone is going to have to deal with it. Whether grounded in bad decisions or uncontrollable forces of nature, this is a messy field full of uncertainty.

Firefighting

Once it hits the fan, how do you handle the problem? Depending on the situation, the solution will vary, but there are a few guidelines that will help you tackle the biggest problems.

The first, and most obvious advice, is to ensure there is a problem. Too often, something gets escalated all the way to the top of the corporate chain with what was believed to be a problem, only to discover it was just someone freaking out and creating a mountain out of a mole hill.

The next piece of advice is one that has been passed down generation to generation: measure twice, cut once. Time after time, people make rash decisions in emergency situations, without fully calculating, or comprehending the situation, only to have the solution to the problem aggravate the situation, or even worse, create more problems! This kind of snowball effect is where I imagine the phrase "when it rains it pours" comes from.

The third piece of advice for fighting fires is ensuring the fire is completely put out. Too often people decide on a quick fix to a problem effectively passing them on for someone else to deal with or delay. Ensuring the fire is completely out means finding the real cause of problems and making sure we address those problems instead of just the symptoms.

Cool Heads

The second most important thing to do when the unexpected happens, is simply keep a cool head. After careful thought and deliberation, I decided to give this topic special attention because of its importance to logistics.

Everybody knows that keeping a cool head in an emergency can be both difficult and extremely rewarding. I will discuss later the subtle effects of remaining calm during logistical crises and methods of actively practicing this essential life skill.

The first adverse effect that comes from panicking is that your view of reality immediately becomes distorted. Acting out of fear or panic will cause you to get caught up in the problem and you won't recognize all the solutions that are available. A decision made during this time will frequently make the problem worse.

A bigger problem with logistical performance anxiety is forgetting to check if it is a problem to begin with. I can't recall how many times I've seen people lose their heads trying to rescue a dropped load, only to find out later that the material wasn't urgent, so they have all the time in the world to get it to its destination.

The final point to keeping your cool is simply avoiding mistakes. Often our emotions lead us to make additional mistakes that aggravate the situation. Making mistakes can make your challenges worse resulting in a downward spiral. Balance of probabilities suggests that while some bad things might happen during one's day, it is probable that the more things go wrong, the more likely they are self-inflicted.

For example, a person wrapped up in a problem, might very easily get careless and spill their coffee, might not realize the speed they're driving, might not follow all the necessary procedures at work, might accidentally lash out at a coworker or a boss and get fired, might forget an important date with their girlfriend and get dumped, might drink too much and get arrested, might forget an important appointment, etc. Understanding this concept and putting it into practice is crucial to logisticians. This lifestyle will devour your will if every time something goes wrong in logistics, you let it take you down a dark spiral. Staying calm is also a good life skill to master. Whether its work or personal problems, the same concept applies.

Learning from Experience

Fail. Adjust. Carry On. Straight forward and simple. The problem with simple advice though, it's easy to ignore and forget. Following are some of the more subtle nuances to how to make learning from experience a solid plan to live by.

Failure is often viewed very negatively by the world. One of the ways to take the negative connotation away is to accept that the world goes on. A fact we knew as children, but over the years have forgotten. As children, we understood that everything we went through was simply a learning experience to prepare us for the future. When we reached adulthood, our expectation usually changes to failure was no longer an option. We frequently exaggerate the seriousness of the situation in our heads without seeing all the facts. This is not to say that some mistakes might bring dire consequences, but the world carries on, adapting to whatever happens in it.

At the end of the day, if you get fired, you'll get a new job. If you drop a shipment, business will continue. If your business bankrupts, you'll start on a new path. The day will start over tomorrow, and a new opportunity will present itself to you. Too many are focused on what happens if the world ends, that they fail to plan for what happens if it just keeps on going.

The logistician's focus should be on a problem bigger problem than the world ending: the world keeps going. The world keeping on will become a bigger problem if we just let our mistakes pile up, escalate, and snowball. So successful people adapt. They take every failure as a learning opportunity, and every mistake as a signal to improve plans and procedures.

There are various paths you can take while learning from your mistakes. A few of the common ones Include:

Learning as you go. Every time you get an undesired result, analyze the problem, come up with a theory, test it on your next round, and continue until the problem is gone. Repeat with every new problem. This procedure can take time, but it's tried and true.

A superior alternative to learning from your mistake would be to learn from other's mistake. By researching, studying, reading, and thinking, you can find other ways to succeed where they failed. This method is the one that saves you the heartache of the learning from the school of hard knocks.

What if your mistakes are not obvious? Complex problems require complex methods of investigation, but once fully understood, they often have simple solutions. Using methods like the five whys, fishbone diagrams, and root cause analysis, might help you narrow in on these types of problems and get you closer to finding that simple solution.

If you can't find a solution to a specific problem, but you've done your research, you worked the problem, and you gave it all you could, then there's always settling for the next best thing. Some problems will not always have the solution you want but may have a variety of solutions with varying degrees of attractiveness to you.

Fail. Adjust. Carry on.

Pitfalls and Errors

Now that we covered making mistakes and emphasized the fact that they should be taken as opportunities to better our processes, it's time to take a closer look at some of the most common mistakes regarding transportation logistics. It is also worth noting that this is the part of the book is where we start getting a bit more technical, however there will be continued emphasis not only the way these issues affect transportation logistics, but also how they can be used to better a person's daily life.

Not Enough Information

The first pitfall has wide implications not only in the transportation fields, but in every other aspect of a person's life. It is the lack of cohesive, thorough information. This issue plagues most businesses, but it's particularly toxic and dangerous for smaller companies...Mistakes can be costly, but the silver lining in this instance is that they are easier to fix in smaller companies than in bigger companies.

What You Don't Know
Might Hurt You

Suppose you are driving down the road, but unbeknownst to you, the bolts on your car's left tire weren't secured properly. Perhaps an experienced driver or mechanic might recognize the slight shake of the car as the wheels struggle against the highway, but most people, especially loud music listeners, might not recognize the subtle signs.

Let's go through a more extreme, but not unheard of, example. Your trucking company has a consolidation truck that goes from Texas to Canada. One of your clients decides to ship explosives with you. Given that you have the proper permits and safeguards, but another company also decides that they want to ship flammable materials on your same consolidation? When I put it in those simple terms, it's easy to see the problem here. Here's when it gets tricky: What if the person loading the truck is a new guy who doesn't know how to read hazardous labels? Or what if it's two different people loading the truck? Or even worse, what if one of those companies accidentally mislabeled their material, so it's not labeled as hazardous? What if the guy who's supposed to be checking for these things (usually the driver) has a new child and he hasn't gotten much sleep?

One of the beauties of transportation logistics is the joint human effort to accomplish a task. In any given transportation request, there is a platoon of people required to move it from point A to point B. The downside to this however is that any mistakes from any of these people could be dangerous or even fatal.

Mistakes Cost Money

The blood of any business is money. Money is what keeps the show running. It's the reason employees show up to work every day. It's the reason other companies agree to do business with you, and it's the reason a company grows and thrives. Mistakes drain bank accounts. Let's say your company hires a brand new, young truck driver without much experience, so you can get away with paying him less than an experienced driver. As he drives his eighteen-wheeler down the road, jerk driver not paying attention cuts in front of him and slams on his breaks. The young truck driver slams on his breaks and turns the truck, flipping it over and hitting multiple other cars. Let's look at all the expenses that might arise from this. First, insurance premium goes up for the company. That is now extra month-to-month money spent. The damaged car drivers sue the company, so the legal fees and settlement costs pile up. That's a lot of extra money. The eighteen-wheeler driver might be fired, so there will be extra costs for hiring and training a new employee. Plus, the costs of any repairs to the company owned vehicles. The government may assess additional fines and fees for perceived violations. There may be additional loss of business arising from the bad press and coverage. I don't have to give you exact amounts to show you that that is a lot of money lost right there, and it wasn't even your driver's mistake. For a smaller or a struggling company this might mean bankruptcy. Your doors would shut down, your employees would lose their jobs, and the business you worked so hard for all your life to build would crumble slowly in front of your eyes.

There's a plethora of TV lawyers that target eighteen wheelers as a primary target of their advertising campaigns. Why? I'm not a lawyer, but if I had to guess, it would be easy money. Eighteen wheelers are expensive, usually the companies who need them have money, and, in one way or another, responsibility could always be blamed on the driver of the big vehicle (unfair as it might be) Multiple arguments against the driver could be used to depict him as the responsible party. Furthermore all the commercial transportation vehicles are required to have insurance, posing the possibility of a big payday by anyone hurt in the incident.

Mistakes cost lives

Using the preceding example, that small mistake in judgement could have very easily turned fatal, and one thing money can't buy is a person's life. Some mistakes might seem unavoidable, or a result of chance, and we might be able to justify those. but when mistakes are made because of lack of information, oversights, and in worse case scenarios, negligence, it is inexcusable; due diligence could have prevented the accident.

Death in the industry is bad for everyone. The company suffers, the coworkers, the public, the fathers, mothers, siblings, and children suffer. Most companies (especially experienced ones) spend large amounts of time and resources training, teaching, and perfecting the processes to avoid as many accidents as possible. This is one of the instances where the interests of the company align with the interest of the employees, and where the most change can be made, because all parties can direct their efforts entirely in one single and unified direction: improvement.

Improvement (even improvement motivated by the fear of death) is good. The concept of improvement is one of the single most powerful concepts known, because it is unique to man. When Darwin wrote <u>Origin of the Species</u>, he couldn't have foreseen the wide range of applications his theory would have or the people it would benefit because ultimately it is not the fittest that survive, but the most adaptable to change. The theory however, after it became more publicly accepted, began to resonate with capitalists. A company must adapt to its environment to thrive and survive, and it can only do so through improvement. This concept isn't exactly mind-blowing to this generation, but it has its place in history among ideas that shaped society.

While I can't cover in this book all the different ways a business can evolve to success, I can state what I consider the highest impact/lowest cost way a business can survive and thrive: fixing the information chain and processes, one of the biggest areas of opportunity and risk that most companies flourish or fall by.

Playing Telephone

Here is what I consider to be the easiest way to prevent most of the issues in logistics: The transfer of information from point source to destination. The world of transportation logistics is often so focused on the product being transported; it forgets about the accompanying information needed to go with it. The information is often an afterthought to the primary cargo being moved. For the football fans in the audience, the cargo can be thought of as the "offense" in your company, your money makers; but to win games, you also need a world class "Defense," which is your information, the resource preventing you from losing money.

The number one way I've seen information deteriorate is through the exchange of hands. If you remember the game of telephone from younger years, this concept is going to sound vaguely familiar. One person whispers in the next person's ear, who in turn whispers it to the next person, and at the end we end up with a convoluted and unrecognizable message from the original. Who would have thought that during the 3rd grade we would experience the main problem that industries continue to struggle with today?

As information passes from one person to another, the message gets distorted. This linear system of information, where different parties hold different parts of the puzzle relevant to final transportation logistics, is inefficient and dangerous, especially if not handled properly. I will be however my own devil's advocate here and say that it does work. Sure, the job gets done this way. It's not completely broken, and some companies do it better than others. This methodology however leaves a big blind spot throughout the supply chain when it comes to vulnerabilities and risk.

Bad Info, Bad Results

The best analogy I can think of to illustrate this flaw is your car. While the old leaky clunker piecemealed together with different junkyard parts might work, there is a more ideal situation. This is the way most companies work. They have a multitude of software badly attached and interfaced together, incoherently trying to communicate with each other. Here is the risk factor: lots of people trying to go on with their day-to-day, stacked against ineffective processes. For example:

A tool breaks at a rig site at midnight and doesn't have a backup. The rig is down, and the company is losing valuable production time and incurring lots of costs. The field engineer runs to his computer and puts in a request for a replacement part to be shipped to him immediately. The warehouse across town where the backup tools are housed is opened from 6:00 a.m. to 5:00 p.m. At 6:00 the first employee walks into the office. He opens his computer the emails start to load, he gets up to get a cup of coffee from the breakroom. On his way back to his desk, he says hi to the rest of the employees walking in to work, makes small talk. When he finally gets to his desk and starts to work, he begins with the emails that came after he left at 5:00 p.m. the previous day. When he finally works through seven hours of emails from last night, he notices the problem. By this time the rig has been down approximately eight hours. The warehouse is also under a strict new policy requiring him to call all the low-cost transportation companies first in order to save the company money. So, he picks up the phone and starts calling the low-cost carriers with low capacity and terrible service, to come get the tool. Perhaps it takes about 30 minutes. Let's pretend here that this is an experienced dispatcher, and nothing goes wrong out of everything that could (system issues, phone issues, mistakes by the trucking company, mistakes by the requestor, etc.) The trucking company picks up the tool and dashes it across town to the wellsite. About 2 hours from loading, delivery, and unloading. Rig down hours tally? About ten-and-a-half hours. Cost of mistake? A few hundred thousand dollars. Number of common-sense things that could have prevented/fixed/controlled this problem? Multiple.

Now let's explore the same problem a few months down the line after a fully integrated process and systems setup is implemented. This is the equivalent of trading in your old clunker for a well-oiled, brand new, high performance car.

A tool breaks down at midnight. The engineer immediately enters the request from the warehouse and follows up via phone with the newly hired overnight warehouse dispatcher. Immediately they call the carrier they KNOW has the trucks on standby for situations like this. A truck is dispatched immediately. It doesn't encounter any traffic picking up or dropping off because it's still night. The tool is at the rig site, which is back up and running in an hour-and-a-half. Despite the hundred dollars a night for the new dispatcher salary and the higher cost of the truck ordered for emergency situations, the new system just saved the company 80% of the rig down costs they suffered in the previous scenario.

Of course, this is not the only way to solve the problem. There are lots of possible solutions to this scenario, ranging from having backup tools for critical processes, all the way to sending a rig worker to pick up the tool themselves; but none of that would have been as dramatic an illustration.

Oftentimes the simplest solutions are the best solutions. However, I've noticed the case with big companies is they can sometimes be a little bulky and locked into their own processes. Going outside of the company to fix the problem can sometimes cause larger issues down the line. For those type of situations, it is often best to get the proper level of management involved in order to effect meaningful change. A hint for all those who aren't entirely used to operational management within big organizations, it is often recommended to frame solutions in terms of money. Once management is aware of how much the inefficiency is costing and how much a solution could save, they'd be more inclined to add it to their busy schedule. Any further advice on this topic might require an entire other book.

The One Who Loses His Head

If you've ever had a job that has an ineffective process, then you understand how difficult and annoying it is to be sitting at your desk trying to do your job, and problems can't be easily moved to a solution stage. Using the above example, If you were the field engineer in the initial situation, you're counting the minutes after the request has been put in, waiting for verification from dispatch. Judging by the math in your head, each passing minute is a few hundred dollars down the drain for the company and possibly means your job. You get desperate. What are your options?

Depending on your situation the options available to you are going to be different. If you recall from the previous chapter, this is where the resourcefulness of an emergency logistician can mean the difference between having a job or not.

This is also the moment where one must be vigilant to avoid further mistakes. Acting under such stress could lead you to make mistakes that aggravate the issue.

One mistake you might make while you're desperately fighting for your job, might be deciding to do the dispatcher's job and call the carrier yourself. This might save you some time, but it might open you up to risk of them getting to a closed warehouse or picking up the wrong tool or getting lost due to incorrect directions or picking a low service carrier that damages the tool on the way to the rig. Damaging or losing the backup tool for a critical operation after the main tool failed would only aggravate the situation further, and while you might say that this is the exception, or that it rarely happens, I'd argue that mistakes like these get more likely the more there is on the line. A small mistake might add a few hundred bucks to the final bill, a big one might add a few hundred thousand. Either way, it's an additional and unnecessary burden.

The resourcefulness and caution that are critical to saving situations like these are the primary reason to keep a cool head, and while I understand that it is harder for some people than others, it is nonetheless a crucial skill that can be diligently and conscientiously practiced.

Unrealistic Expectations

Unrealistic expectations are the most common cause of communication issues. There are a few reasons for this. The first is that everyone has different frames of reference that affect their perception of a problem. Here's an exercise that I came across at a leadership seminar a few years back: If you instruct a room full of people to blow up a balloon to a medium size, the result would be that everyone ends up with varying size balloons. Everyone has a different understanding of the word medium, and there is no specific frame of reference involved other than their own experiences. As a leader, if you give an instruction, and the results are varied like in the balloon example, it stands to reason that instead of getting angry at your employees for getting different results, you should reframe your instructions more clearly and with more guidance. For example, a more accurate way to instruct the room regarding the balloons, would be to instruct the room to blow the balloon to the size of a melon. The more precise instruction would lower the size variations as people try to get it closer to the size of a melon. This won't make the instruction perfect, but it is a way to start understanding expectations in the context of instruction and error variability.

Understanding expectations in the context of instruction and error variability has two major implications. The first is that we begin to understand the control points we have available for the outcome of the interaction. The second implication is that we can use this as a starting point of analysis of all the things that could go wrong, and we can begin to maneuver against them.

Most people will see the stark difference when we put it in a social context. When you tell a large group of people that a party starts at 8:00 pm., only a minor portion of them will show up at 8:00 p.m., while the majority will show up between 8:15 p.m. and 10:00 p.m. If, however, you tell an equally large number of people that their job interviews start at 8:00 a.m., most people will show up between 7:30 a.m. to 7:55 a.m. While most people would be quick to attribute this to context, and they would be partially right, we can't ignore the variability that correlates with different understandings of the expectation that frames the request.

The Boss Isn't Always Right

You know it, I know it, the world knows it, your boss is not always right. Your boss might not even be right most of the time, that's why this next section is going to be very important. There are a few key elements that most people notice are at play when interacting with superiors at work. The first elephant in the room is that displeasing your boss might lead to an extended vacation down at the unemployment line. That alone will lead most people to shift their behavior, either out of fear or understandable caution.

The next dynamic is the tendency to believe they know better than you. Perhaps due to seniority in the company, or simply position. In theory, bosses get paid more because they are supposed to know more, which is not always the case. It's interesting to see this dynamic break down when the employee has the seniority or both people began working at the same company at the same time.

The next dynamic when dealing with a superior is simply a matter of common sense. When we talk to our superiors, some of us tend to exaggerate the accomplishments and downplay our mistakes and flaws to portray ourselves in a better light. There is nothing wrong with that, but we need to be cognizant of it for reason to be explained shortly.

Disclaimer: Following my advice might get you fired if followed incorrectly, consider yourself warned, and please take into consideration all the details before going around waving my advice like a toddler running with scissors.

Having an honest relationship with your boss makes the following tips easier to follow. I know that not everybody has this, or has hope for it, in which case my advice will be harder to implement, but it is still worth implementing as much as the relationship allows.

Being a "yes man" can get you into a lot of trouble by pressuring you to agree to impossible tasks doomed to fail. Instead of always saying yes and putting yourself under immense stress only to fail in the end, spend time working on recognizing no-win situations and steering away from those.

If you're a young professional at a new company working logistics, I'd suggest relying on your experienced coworkers for advice. There might be instances where your boss asks you to do something impossible. As tactfully as possible, let him know your concerns and ask for advice and resources to either accomplish what they asked of you or shift the expectations from the start about what is possible. Taking your boss's word as gospel, will lead to a lot of stressful nights and terrible mornings.

Frequently, you and your superior will have conflicting goals. While this topic alone would take an entire book in game theory to understand, I'll attempt to summarize the dynamic purposes of this book. As a logistics specialist, your goal might just be to move freight from point A to point B. While for your boss this might be a secondary priority. His first priorities might be keeping the business afloat, acquiring new customers, growing the business, or managing their projects. In the instance you're a small business owner who is their own boss who must handle your own logistics, EVERYTHING STILL APLIES! Always question yourself. Before you promise a delivery date to your customer, ask yourself if this is logistically, legally, and financially feasible. While some things might be feasible one way, they may not be in another.

What is Possible vs. What is Feasible

Let's talk about a big problem in logistics, the possible vs. the feasible. It is in fact possible to move 45,000 lbs. (22.5 tons) of products from Houston, Texas, to Prudhoe Bay, Alaska, overnight for a few hundred thousand dollars. It would be an absolute miracle of the human ability to be able to pull off such a thing. Chances are, however, for most companies that level of service is simply not worth wrecking the bottom line; it is financially unfeasible.

According to Google maps, that same trip over the road should take you 80 hours or 3.3 days and it would cost you between $10,000 and $20,000. This might be an easier burden for the company to bear, but if I allow exactly 80 hours to move that much weight from Houston to Prudhoe Bay, I can guarantee that it will always be late. In addition, we would be ignoring Department of Transportation (DOT) restrictions that prohibit single driver operated commercial vehicles to drive over eleven hours straight, before having to rest for ten. This is now enforced with electronic logs, so the eighty-hour drive solution is not legally feasible.

Once the mandatory legal breaks are calculated, we'd be looking closer to 150 or 6.3 days. For the sake of argument, let's discuss a slightly more expensive option of meeting the deadline. Some big trucks have a sleeping compartment, so they could be driven by a team of drivers. This would circumvent the DOT restriction of having to stop every 11 hours and takes us back to the 80-hour trip scenario. Even with team drivers, this trip is not feasible in 6.3 days due to the last and often forgotten characteristic of logistics: the people factor.

Basic personal needs (bathroom breaks, breakfast, lunch, dinner, showering, stretching, and others)in addition to road conditions, traffic, weather, border inspections, gas stops, loading and unloading times, unexpected police inspections, flat tires, etc. are factors that would add in a time variable to be considered. So, while team drivers would make it legally and financially feasible, it would not be logistically feasible, unless we consider all the necessary non-negotiable time added activities this would require.

Even google maps adds a disclaimer with this route: "These directions are for planning purposes only. You may find that construction projects, traffic, weather, or other events may cause conditions to differ from the map results, and you should plan your route accordingly. You must obey all signs or notices regarding your route."

So here are the basic questions to keep in mind when planning things like this:

1. Is it physically possible to do?
2. Is it legal to do?

3. Can I afford to do it?
4. What all can stop me or slow me down while I'm doing it?

After you've answered those 4 questions the rest are going to be technicalities. I'll elaborate on this topic a bit later to drill down further into all the technicalities and nuances. I'll also include a few supporting documents at the end of the book for reference.

The Cost of Getting it Done

"If you can measure it, you can control it." That's one popular cliché running amok in most businesses. The bigger the business the more attractive putting a figure to everything is; and as I've come to find out, this is often not entirely accurate for various reasons:

The first and biggest issue is human error. People often get so wrapped up in putting numbers on everything so it will look good to their superiors, that they often go for easiest numbers to obtain, instead of relevant numbers. People automatically filter numbers that make them look good and manicure them to look even better. Only when there is an obvious problem, do people seem to take a more honest look at the numbers long enough to find something to point the finger at, instead of understanding how all the pieces and numbers fit together.

Imagine your manager walking into a monthly meeting saying "Team, I have good news, I found a way to save this company thousands of dollars." If you're like me, your first thought is going to be "What fresh hell is this," because in my mind there are only a few easy ways to eliminate thousands of dollars a year:

1. Get rid of various employees, lowering morale
2. Use cheaper materials, lowering the quality of the

overall product

3. Use cheaper transportation, lowering customer service and delivery
4. Use cheaper software, often leading to attrition and change management problems
5. Remove work perks and things that increase employee morale

In the manager's mind, he might be walking out with an extremely good piece of news that should earn him a bonus for meeting some ambiguous corporate guideline he's forced to abide by. He'll give out an order about the new way things are going to be, and all his employees are going to be forced to deal with whatever fallout this new cost-cutting strategy will bring into their lives.

I am by no means saying that cutting costs is bad. It benefits everyone involved to run a lean company that only uses what it needs to get the job done. However, my faith in people isn't optimistic by default. There is a very strong possibility that this manager's entire decision was made simply for the measurable dollar amount he would be saving at the expense of every other immeasurable aspect of whatever job is being affected. This was an obvious and easy example to begin making this point, so we'll move on to something a bit more complex:

Let's assume at your company you have a team of people who plan shipments from your distribution centers to your retail stores. They get a request from various locations across the states, and the planners find a nearby hub with product, call a trucking company, and order the product to be picked up and delivered to the location that needs it.

You, as a manager, decide the company is always using the expensive carriers instead of the cheaper ones. You implement a cost-cutting strategy, challenging your team to use the cheapest trucking companies whenever possible. As a result, your team spends more time on average calling trucking companies to get lower bids.

Now you realize that your planners at taking too long planning shipments and your customers have complained about quality issues. You look at some measurements, and you find out that, on average, it takes planners about 20 minutes to plan any given shipment; so you put a new mandate out, that all shipments must be planned within 20 minutes arrival. Your planners will do two things. First, they won't search for the lowest cost now because that takes too long. Instead, they'll just search for a cost "low enough," raising the cost of transportation again. Secondly, they'll leave the shipments they recognize as more difficult to someone else on the team, causing some shipments to ultimately be ignored.

When you notice what is happening, you automatically assign all the shipments evenly and chronologically, so the planners address all the shipments and an even workload is created. Your slower planners will suffer because they have daily shipments piling up, while the more experienced planners are sitting there bored at their desks, also causing shipments get dropped by the slower planners that could have easily been addressed by the more experienced ones.

So, what is the solution? There isn't one specific solution to problems like this, mostly because they bring complex and often unforeseen consequences. What I can suggest is to deeply analyze the repercussions of any decisions you make. When you're about to deliver a change of direction, procedure, or policy, sit quietly for a few minutes and imagine life from the shoes of every single person that will be affected by this. If you don't know how it will affect most people, then there is a very large possibility your new rule will only fix the problem by creating others. An alternate solution for the issue might have gone something like this:

After the mandate was issued to spend time cutting costs, a twin mandate should have been given increasing the headcount by one to offset the loss of quality for each shipment. Considering that the extra work was going to slow down workers and the salary of one extra employee was less than the expected cost savings achieved by the first mandate, this solution might have prevented further problems caused by management's own actions.

The biggest problem however with the example is the company loss of motivated employees. Constantly changing and conflicting rules lower company morale through the constant stress of change. The effectiveness of the entire company drops by focusing entirely on lowering one easily measurable metric at the expense of all the others.

What Needs to be Moved?

Now it's time to get more technical. If you were simply looking for life advice from a Logistics specialist, you can pretty much stop reading now. If you're looking for more, and don't mind the technical details coming up, then you should continue reading. If you're reading this book for your job, your industry, or your career in general, then you should keep reading, as I cover some of the finer nuances of the industry and emphasize relevant common-sense points often forgotten. As always, common sense is a useful skill to develop, so you'll have plenty to learn, even if the details don't exactly apply to your current needs.

Now that we've established some common mindset, assumptions, perspectives, and general things to watch out for, let's continue the drill down process by moving on to the next logical step in our logistics journey to the crucial question "What are we moving?"

The reason this question is important should be obvious, but in case it isn't, let's consider some of the possible derivative questions that need to be answered first.

- How much space do I need?
- How much weight do I need to consider?
- What is the best mode of transport?
- What precautions do I need to take for the safe

transport of the product?
- What precautions do I need to take for the safety of all those involved in the movement?
- What legal and financial guidelines apply?
- What challenges am I going to find while trying to move this?
- Is this a strategic move, or a transactional move?
- What loading and offloading requirements are applicable?

As you can see, the question "What are we moving" is particularly deceptive because it summarizes all the questions, we really need to know in one simple question. For example, let's say you're moving a crate of watermelons.

- How much space do I need?
  - Crate dimensions are often 4 x 4 x 4 feet.
- How much weight do I need to consider?
  - Often about 1,000 lbs.
- What is the best mode of transport?
  - Truck for short distances, Less Than Truckload (LTL) for longer distances
- What precautions do I need to take for the safe transport of the product?
  - Crate on pallet for easy forklift handling
- What precautions do I need to take for the safety of all those involved in the movement?
  - Clearly marked weight and handling warnings clear on box
- What legal and financial guidelines apply?
  - U.S. Food and Drug Administration Guidelines
- What challenges am I going to find while trying to move this?
  - Time constraints for produce freshness

- Is this a strategic move, or a transactional move?
    - Transactional for produce sellers, possible strategic for a festival planner
- What loading and offloading requirements are applicable?
    - Possibly a forklift

TYPES OF PRODUCTS

A subsection of the question "What are we shipping" that deserves special attention is the eventuality that whatever you are shipping contains dangerous goods. As you may imagine, these types of moves require special attention. The government pays extra attention to these products, and so should you. I won't go into all the technicalities of the subject, but I will highlight a few that should not be ignored. I will also include some resources at the end of the book so you can follow those leads if this section applies to you.

Hazardous and Dangerous Moves

The first step towards identifying and preventing these kinds of issues, would be to know your product. While some items might be common sense dangerous like dynamite, gasoline, and uranium, there are a lot of everyday use products not easily recognized as hazardous materials, such as mouthwash and nail polish (Flammable Liquids class 3), Batteries (Class 8 Corrosive materials), anything pressurized (Explosive), and fertilizer (Class 5 Oxidizers and Organic Peroxides). Researching before shipping anything new should be the standard practice.

A second variable in hazardous or dangerous moves would be quantities shipped. There will be many non-hazardous materials that can ship fine alone but have a critical quantity in which they would be considered hazardous.

If you're shipping internationally, you should also be aware of what is considered Dual Use Goods. These are goods classified as civilian goods, but with possible military applications.

Alongside this note, I'd like to point out that when dealing with foreign countries, all export and import restrictions should be observed.

Every hazardous product should come with a Hazardous Material Safety Data Sheet from the manufacturer that can give you an overview of the product, the risks, the appropriate regulatory codes (UN Number, HTS Codes, ECCN, etc.), the labeling, packaging, and the response procedures necessary.

Packaging

If you must ship hazardous materials, and you're aware the kind of hazards they present, the next step is to properly package and label the material. This part is particularly important for two main reasons. Proper packaging means decreased risk of something going wrong during transport. That alone could save you a lot of headaches as far as actually causing some disaster down the road. At the least, proper labeling and documentation will prevent you from getting fines, which is a nice benefit. However, the main reason you want to properly label the shipment is to ensure first responders can be effective in case something does go wrong down the road. Accidents are bad in and of themselves but imagine the field day the lawyers are going to have with your company if your lack of attention aggravated the problem for the government, first responders, and ultimately the citizens. One mishandled accident could turn your successful company into a bankruptcy case.

Governments and Permits

As you may have noticed, the government has a vested interest in whatever it is you're doing, especially on a commercial platform. "I didn't know" is not a good legal defense and will not stop the government from bankrupting you with fines for knowingly or unknowingly breaking the law. Researching every aspect of the law pertaining to your own business should be a priority and cannot be ignored if you hope to stay in business for the long term. At the very minimum, following all government regulations and procedures will save you a lot of money in fines, but these regulations are ultimately meant to save lives.

If you plan on shipping a variety of items, I'd suggest attending a few extra classes and getting a few hazardous materials certifications to sharpen your understanding of the products you're shipping and why they're dangerous.

My personal favorite resource for hazardous materials reference is **the Hazmat 49 CFR Parts 100-185.**

For more information regarding these or any other hazardous material requirements visit www.phmsa.dot.gov.

I don't expect you to become a hazardous material expert. To truly understand all the nuances required for the transportation of hazardous materials requires years and years of work and experience. I do encourage you to learn and educate yourself as much as possible regarding the products you ship, however. Your company should also keep in mind there are 3rd party companies that dedicate themselves exclusively to the counsel, management, and education of companies on hazardous material transportations. These experts can advise your company regarding packaging, labeling, and transporting all your materials, and they can help you deal with emergencies as they arise.

You can also outsource the managing, handling, and transporting entirely to a 3rd party company. If this is a risk for your company, I'd recommend exploring ALL options, and find out what is best for your case.

Special Needs

Products don't need to be hazardous to have special needs and requirements. A company that dedicates themselves to creating and selling customized ice sculptures for various events doesn't necessarily need to pass much government regulation to transport ice sculptures across town, but they might need, at minimum, a refrigerated truck to ensure the sculpture gets to its destination intact during a hot summer day and at a maximum, some liquid nitrogen (hazardous material) on board. This will affect the types of decisions you need to make. There are also some chemicals, that need to be kept at warm temperatures to prevent spoilage If your main client is in Alaska, there might be a need for a temperature control vehicle to make the trip instead of a regular truck.

Food and produce might also need to be transported in temperature-controlled vehicles, as well as follow other Food and Drug Administration requirements. If the product needs to travel upright, ensuring that the companies can accommodate that will be crucial and must be thought of and planned.

Other types of special needs might have to do with the loading and unloading locations. A loading location might be planning to load the materials with a crane, so a box van would make it impossible to load. The unloading destination might not have a forklift to unload material, so special arrangements need to be made to accommodate for it.

If your material is hazardous, the shipment might not be compatible to travel with other hazardous materials. Loading explosives and flammable materials in one truck does not necessarily mean they'll explode, and perhaps 95% of the time they won't, but the disaster caused by them in case they do could be catastrophic. There are regulations to prevent that kind of disaster, including a list of products that should not under any circumstance travel together.

Weight and Dimensions

The next thing to consider, when trying to move any product, whether oil and gas tools, produce, emergency supplies, or construction materials, is the weight and dimensions of what you're trying to move. Again, while this may seem like common sense to just about everyone, just like the previously deceptive question of "What are we shipping," this one has implications that come along with whatever answer is given.

- Are the dimensions correct?
- What equipment is necessary to move this?
- Is this material stackable or not?
- Will I need any oversized permits?
- Can this go in a smaller vehicle with acceptable overhang?
- Will the dimensions affect my trucking options?

The first and second points I've made on that list, are particularly relevant when it comes to transportation for one simple reason: the "screw it" principle. It is quite common in most industries to not know the exact weight of things, so oftentimes someone at the company eyeballs the material and says, "Screw it, it's about ____ lbs. It can fit on ____ truck". This isn't much of an issue when particularly experienced employees do it or when it's easy to calculate, but it can cause big issues when new employees trying to cut costs do it.

Take for example a 1 x1 x 1 ft., 5lb. box. This particularly small box could probably be transported on the back of a motorcycle. You could put it in the passenger side of your car. You could throw it on the back of a truck. You could transport it in an airplane (provided there aren't any other travel restrictions). You might ship it in a one-ton truck or even an eighteen-wheeler. A smaller object being carried in big trucks is not a problem in the least. However, the inverse scenario of this is another story.

All shipments will have a minimum acceptable transportation method. For example, a single 4 x4 ft. pallet can probably be carried on a one ton truck. Pallets, however, can vary wildly on weight, depending on what they're carrying. If it's below certain weight, it could be carried on a pickup truck.

A 500 lb. drilling tool would perfectly meet a pickup truck's weight capacity. However, if it's a 20-30 ft. long tool, it might be illegal to transport it on a pickup truck because of potential traffic hazards.

That is why it's important first to try to get the estimations as accurate as possible, and if it's not possible, then it's recommended to overestimate the weight rather than underestimate it.

The next question might be "Is it stackable?" Stackable material can usually fetch lower transportation costs when shipping Less Than Truckload (LTL), but it is not recommended for delicate products or oddly shaped ones. A square pallet full of brick is stackable, but an oddly shaped engineering measurement tool might not be.

If the product is too big, we might run into two other issues: the equipment necessary to move it and required legal permits. Perhaps you've been lucky enough to see this while you're driving down the highway: a house mounted on the back of on an eighteen-wheeler driving down the middle of two lanes. Usually it's accompanied by a car in front of it with a tall flag to make sure it doesn't hit anything. Sometimes it even has police escort and a big banner to remind you that it is an oversized load (in case you couldn't already tell from the massiveness of the entire thing). To get permission to move that house, someone had to ask the government.

Sometimes the same "screw it" people from above, in order to try to save a few bucks, will try to push the limits of certain equipment. For example, a regular pickup truck might be a lot cheaper than a 1-ton truck, which is of course cheaper than a truck with trailer (known as Minifloat in some industries), which is cheaper than an eighteen wheeler. Sometimes people at the shop might say, "Screw it. just tie it good, put it on a regular truck, and put a flag on it." While that might work in some instances, there is just so much of that you can get away with before you get stuck with a fine more expensive than it would have been to get a slightly bigger truck for the move.

All the previously mentioned issues are mild compared to the possible repercussions of not paying proper attention to dims and weights. Take for example, an eighteen-wheeler carrying an illegally heavy load. They might start driving down the road with no more issues than a strained truck and lower fuel efficiency. However, the heavier the truck is, the harder it would be to stop in an emergency, which could cause bigger problems, including loss of life. If a load is top heavy, the truck might flip over taking a sharp turn; if it is too tall, the truck might hit the underpass; if there is too much overhang, it might hit other travelers on the road.

WHAT IS THE BEST
WAY TO MOVE IT?

So far, we've covered mindsets we need to have going in to managing transportation logistics, and we've covered the "what" that encompasses the different considerations we need in order to understand the products we're trying to move. Now, it's time to approach the next step, the all-important "how."

How Far Does it Need to Go?

The origin and destinations are crucial when it comes to transportation, as they alone will bring about some restrictions and possibilities that make the transportation selection a little easier. For example, I can't transport anything from San Francisco to Hawaii via truck, so when I'm looking at all the transportation companies that can help me carry my product, I'll immediately eliminate the ones that don't have air, or vessel services. This means two things: with good planning in advance, this could turn out to be a very cost-effective move of materials. With bad planning, this could turn out very expensive. If you're only moving a few things across towns, it most likely will be less expensive to move, since I won't have to worry about sea or air freight. This would also significantly narrow my options as well.

Local Runs

Depending on where you live, local runs are probably the easiest ones to deal with. Most of these would be same day deliveries. If we're talking about a small business with relatively constant shipping needs, the best bet might be a company truck to make regular deliveries. It will be more cost effective in the long run, and your costs would be limited to the investment on the truck, maintenance, and gas. If the small business doesn't have enough regular shipping needs, it might be best to shop around different local trucking companies to move your product at a cost per mile or per run. These trucking companies usually have different types of equipment to fit your needs and usually give you a good deal if you work regularly with them. For example, if you have a grocery store where most of your products are delivered straight to your door by a grocery wholesaler, then you might save yourself a lot of money by hiring a truck as you need it for any needed big moves you might have to make, like furniture, shelves, and equipment.

Is the Move Across States?

Shipping things across states is where things begin to get interesting. This is usually when cost becomes more of a priority, as every move becomes more expensive. Keeping your product and dimensions in mind, our options begin to open from air, sea (Alaska and Hawaii), and land. At this point of the transportation decisions, the required delivery date and good planning begin to pay off.

If your product is small, non-hazardous, and needs to travel a long distance relatively quickly, the cheapest options are usually big companies, such as the United States Postal Service, Fedex, or

UPS.

If the product gets bigger than 150 lbs., then freight options come into play. Fedex Freight, UPS Freight, Saia Motor Freight services, and Levinge usually take a few days to consolidate all the shipments into one truck, drive them to their closest hub, sort by closest hub near destination, drive the consolidated truck to the next hub, and deliver it in some of their local trucks to their final destination. These services vary from next day for short distances to a week or two across the country. Depending on their dimensions and weight, different LTL (spell out first use of LTL) carriers would be able to handle your shipments. Always verify the dimensions with the carriers before dispatching them for your load as they all have different size and weight restrictions.

The next step up in this category is a dedicated truck for two main reasons. The first is the level of control you want to have over your shipment. Each business is different, and it might not make sense for your business to consolidate a product with a lot of other things from different companies. The second reason is that even these companies are still too slow and your product needs to move urgently. Moving freight to a neighboring state can be done in an emergency by a dedicated truck. The department of transportation currently has an 11-hour straight drive restriction on commercial truck drivers, which means any place within a 10-hour radius (1 hour as buffer for loading and unloading) is fair game for same day or immediate delivery. Unless you live in Texas or Alaska, this is usually enough time to get you a few states over in a hurry. At this point, hiring a truck with the necessary space to move your material and paying them to drive straight through might be your best option.

Is it Across Countries?

As if things aren't difficult enough, international shipments add a new level of complexity. Depending on origin and destination, these shipments will have a variety of requirements and complexities unique to each country. Transportation will no longer require the involvement of one government, but multiple.

Countries connected by land, can be treated as regular land shipments. For example, a truck picking up materials in the United States can deliver the shipment straight to Canada. The main differences are the vehicle must travel through customs and provide the proper documentation for cross-border shipments, with everything regarding the shipment properly documented, labeled, recorded to the dollar value, and exact specifications. The details regarding country export and import laws must be consulted and verified for every shipment regularly, as embargo and law changes can quickly change depending on the country's political climate. Once the cargo has acquired the proper greenlights from both countries, the cargo can be legally transported.

For most companies, it is advised they hire either consultants or a 3rd party export specialist to handle the legal and logistical aspects for each shipment to leverage their contacts and expertise for low costs solutions.

Is it Across the Sea?

The only differences in shipping something across continents over just countries are the bigger logistics issues. Third party companies are adept at handling these types of issues. However, a few words of advice on this topic: Things happen (yes, again as it is important to reiterate). As much as companies can "guarantee" a required delivery date, the more moving pieces there are in any shipment, the more things can go wrong. If possible, always try to hedge against uncertainty with extra time buffers. Suppose the two methods the shipment can move now would be by sea or air. With enough planning, an intermodal shipping option would be the most cost-effective method to move large amounts of freight. However the importance of air cannot be underestimated. The most crucial aspect in this scenario would be a break-even analysis on the cost of moving freight by either method, hedged against the overall cost of the shipment and the importance of getting it to where it needs to be by a specific date.

How Fast Does it Need to Go?

Now that we've covered a couple of the most crucial concepts, it's time to revisit one of the ones I previously mentioned in this book. The nuances that come with meeting a deadline can be a monstrous beast to tame. While simply reading this book will not guarantee you always make your deliveries, I hope it will severely shorten the learning curve by providing reinforced concepts to remember while doing your job. Now, let's revisit the three biggest hurdles logisticians need to be aware of for each shipment they schedule:

The rule of thumb I've created to calculate time:
Estimated Transit time = Physical Time + Average Delays (Legal & Physical),
IF legally and financially feasible

The following example shows the physical, financial, and legal restrictions we must keep in mind to make any accurate calculations and promises to our customers and be able to live up to them.

You've got a full truckload (approximately 44,000 lbs.) of electronics to move from Palo Alto, California, to a warehouse in Houston, Texas. The dispatcher Jason, sources a local truck to do the job.

Google Maps Estimated Drive Time = 28 Hours

- 1 hour for the truck to arrive
- 30 minutes for Johnny to load the truck
- 7 ½ hours driving
- 1 hour food breaks & gas
- 11 hour DOT mandated reset
- 8 more hours driving
- 1 hour customs stop (if they drive by El Paso)
- 1 hour food break & gas
- 11 hour DOT mandated reset
- 8 more hours of drive
- 1 hour food break and gas
- 1 hour traffic delays
- 11 hour DOT mandated reset
- 4 ½ more hours driving
- 30 minute traffic delays
- 30 minutes to unload at facility

Calculated total transport time: 68 hours and 30 minutes, almost 2½ times longer than originally expected. This is considering a standard drive. Any delays, traffic congestion, accidents, and mistakes would only make it longer. Let's say the dispatcher Jason is absent a few days on a family emergency and a new guy takes his place. If he doesn't know better, he might dispatch something according to Google and the materials will arrive a whole day later than he promised.

Physically Possible

Is it physically possible? Let's face it, Amazon Prime has us spoiled. Google has got us accustomed to look at an "optimal" route by which to make our plans, and with the Internet, everything seems to be getting faster and faster. In managing materials though, it is important to understand all the processes that must take place in order to make accurate plans that will affect the business bottom line. I cannot emphasize enough the importance of knowledge.

Now to the original question : Is it physically possible? The answer to that in this instance, is in 28 Hours. It IS possible to make the drive in 28 Hours, but it doesn't mean that the shipment will arrive in 28 hours. In a theoretical future, a self-driving car, without the 11-hour DOT restriction, the need for food, and a super-efficient gas tank, could physically move the product in 28 hours, assuming current infrastructure and ignoring loading and unloading times. This might be where the transportation industry is currently heading, but it just isn't quite there yet.

However, if you have a cross-town shipment in Houston, Texas, on a truck you own that is already loaded with the material, you can rely on Google Maps to provide a relatively accurate drive time to your destination.

Every case is going to be different, and perhaps with a little experience we could get better at foreseeing most scenarios, but the first step in the calculation for delivery times is what is physically possible. No shipment should ever be promised before what is physically possible. People who oversee sales and/ or making commitments on behalf of the company should be painfully aware of all these nuances.

Legally Possible

Government's role in business can be boiled down to one word, regulation. It is the responsibility of the government to create laws to safeguard the population against possible harm from careless, dangerous, and harmful business practices. This often comes at the cost of many efficiencies that businesses have adapted over time to resolve day to day problems and regain a competitive edge.

I've mentioned a few times here the DOT regulation that requires all commercial transport vehicles to stop after ten hours and rest for eleven. This regulation was put in place to minimize the number of eighteen-wheeler accidents resulting from overworked truck drivers falling asleep at the wheel. Now, this rule has been around for a little while, but in 2018, a monitoring system was put in place to prevent truck drivers from circumventing the rules and keep them accountable. While it might be better for a company if a truck could drive 24 hours without stopping, and perhaps even for the driver, if the company was willing to pay for it, the increased risk to the population calls for legal action and government involvement.

For cross country movements, there's an extra level of security. The U.S. Customs and Border Protection safeguards the country from illegal cargo entering the country, and most other countries have equivalent agencies. These arose from increased illegal imports into the country. This level of governmental protection can slow down business and cut into the companies' profits in exchange for population security.

A common and little thought of example is importing food products from overseas. Restaurants have been known to lose millions for their imported food products due to them being held at the border for extended periods of time until the shipment eventually reaches the expiration date. The USDA has regulation and guidelines that dictate the proper classifications, packaging, and clearing of goods for transport into the United States. This may also seem like a blow to the United States businesses trying to import food from other countries, but ultimately this regulation is to attempt to safeguard the United States from different diseases common across other parts of the world. While restaurants are missing out on delicious exotic imported salami, these regulations attempt to safeguard the United States from diseases that might have infected the cattle or swine from the product was processed from. The laws must be obeyed for the welfare of the population; however, being aware of all the laws pertaining to the products you're transporting will go a long way toward ensuring you make accurate and profitable decisions. The lack of knowledge in these circumstances could lead to loss of business, fines, and in extreme circumstances, jail. Things as simple as aerosols, lithium batteries, and food could lead to business-stopping problems in your supply chain.

Using the example above, a truckload of electronics containing lithium batteries would require a hazardous materials driver, as well as proper packaging, identification, and placarding of the vehicle to be legal for transport.

Financially Possible

Money makes the cargo go around. The truck drivers out in the world are driving trucks for one primary reason, because they have bills to pay. Chances are if you're getting a college degree, or starting a business, it's because you're hoping to bring more money into your life. The reason why it is possible to ask a person to leave their home and family behind to drive a week across the country and back is because they're getting paid enough for it. The more you ask for, the more you pay. Now let's start with the financial product mix. Let's say that each unit costs $10 dollars to make. A pallet of 500 Units makes that $5,000 dollars to move. If you sell each item at $11 dollars (Assuming they don't sell for more than that), you'll make $5,500 dollars in revenue per pallet, turning $500 in profit for each pallet or $12,000 for each truckload of these electronics (24 standard size pallets) that you sell. For argument's sake, let's assume that this is an urgent order and the client can't wait for the previously calculated 68 plus hours. Either you get it to them faster, or you lose all future business with this client. What do you do?

You can't fly this, as it contains lithium batteries, and it would probably cost way too much to charter a plane for a move like this ($50,000 plus at the cheapest). You can't endorse illegal driving practices, or you might lose a lot more than the business. What you can do is hire team drivers. Two drivers to drive the eighteen-wheeler, which must have a dedicated DOT approved sleeper cab to allow the truck to be driven continuously, minus food and gas stops, without the mandated 11-hour break (other rules still apply). Since the two drivers can take turns sleeping and resting while the other drives, this is a viable choice. While many other things may delay it further from the physically possible 28-hour drive, it should significantly reduce the previously estimated 68 hours.

The standard cost for a move like this would be approximately $4,500 dollars with single drivers. Assuming a markup for team drivers at around 30-40% (the second driver must get paid too), it might put us closer to $6,000 THAT IS HALF OF THE ORIGINAL ESTIMATED PROFITS!

I'm not saying that this will be the case for everything that gets shipped, and a clever company might add the expected cost of transportation per unit to the original cost-per-unit analysis to get a more accurate cost per unit for its calculations. My point here would be to take costs like these into consideration, as they are obviously crucial to the bottom line. In this scenario, I'd advise to add the average expected cost of transportation to the original cost per unit analysis and to understand the importance of how longer planning has a direct effect on the bottom line to maximize cost avoidance and improve overall company profitability.

What do You Need to Move It?

With a better understanding of the weight requirements and trucks, let's dive a bit further into the physical requirements of moving certain items. For example, as strong as I think I might be, human limits extend only to a certain degree. At the time I wrote this book, one of my favorite Game of Thrones actors Hafþór Björnsson had a world record of deadlifting 1,041 lbs.

About the same time, I coordinated the overnight movement of a pallet of oilfield tools weighing around the same amount from Houston, Texas, to Midland, Texas, approximately 500 miles away. I along with an entire crew of players, equipment, and overseeing regulatory bodies, were able to easily and efficiently accomplish something that is considered impossible by pure human physical ability standards. This isn't to try to downplay Hafþór Björnsson's accomplishments but shows the amazing results of human capabilities and efficiencies achieved by collaboration and coordination.

Having said all this, it is important to account for the proper resources to continue to accomplish these feats.

After it's physically, financially, and legally possible to do so, let's examine the "how" in order to take it from a theoretical exercise to a physical one. There are two primary considerations, weight and size. Weight and size let us narrow the types of vehicles necessary for the transportation of our cargo to a specific one or two.

Remember, that the primary assumption here is that we want to minimize the cost of the shipment by only paying for the absolute minimum space we need in any given situation. This strategy may change given a different set of parameters and exceptions. The standard eighteen-wheeler van trailer has a 48 ft. long bed, 8 ft. wide by 9 ft. high, and it can carry approximately 45,000 lbs. As with cars, there's all types, models, and variances, so this is just an example. Doing your research and having an open conversation with your desired carrier would give you an accurate perspective of the costs and options available for your type of shipment.

Even if you've got the lifting aptitude of Hafþór Björnsson, chances are you're going to need help to load and unload most commercial shipments. Some carriers will offer loading and unloading services for you, but not all, so make sure to bring up this point, when having a conversation with the carriers. Most commonly, the carrier's responsibility is to show up, wait to get loaded, drive to the destination, wait to get unloaded, and get the paperwork signed. Anything after that is considered extra services.

This means two things: It's up to the origin to have everything necessary to load up the truck and it's up to the destination to unload the truck, so it's important to consider what you have available. For things like pallets, a small forklift can do the job; for bigger items such as pipe or drilling motors, it might be best to have a flat deck truck transport them and a crane to drop them on the truck carefully. This means sometimes renting out a forklift or a crane for specific jobs, a practice that comes with its own logistics problems.

An afterthought for many shippers, dunnage, straps, tarps, etc. should also be considered, basically anything necessary to secure the materials to the truck so they can be safely transported. We've all seen the nightmare videos of pieces flying out of cargo trucks into windshields, pipes coming unstrapped crushing nearby vehicles, and massive accidents caused by unaware cargo drivers dropping debris on the highway.

Such afterthoughts are cause for millions of dollars and productive hours lost in the transportation industry.   For example, you have an urgent shipment that must deliver 8 hours away. You order a truck, and it arrives within an hour (1 hour). After loading the truck (30 minutes), you find out that it doesn't have the proper dunnage to secure the load. While it's being unloaded (30 minutes), the driver takes off to the nearby truck stop to buy some extra items (30 minutes). Afterwards, the load gets reloaded and secured properly enough to travel (30 more minutes). Three hours later, the driver only has seven hours to complete an eight-hour trip. Hence the shipment will now arrive 19 hours later due to the DOT regulations, instead of the previously calculated eight.

Just like that, lots of unproductive time, dropped promises, and millions of dollars in losses and non-performance fines pile up unnecessarily in company general ledgers every year.

Another regular issue in transportation, particularly with cross-border shipments, is the problem of paperwork. A single piece of paper with incorrect information could delay your shipment for weeks and cost you thousands, depending on the situation.

ACCURATE PAPERWORK IS CRUCIAL!!

A thorough inspection of all necessary paperwork should be mandatory for all cross-border shipments. One of my personal proposed solutions for this issue is a data package, which I'll address in more detail later in the book.

CARRIER SELECTION

Now that we've put a full picture together of what we need, including origin to destination, required delivery date, equipment, and avoided some common pitfalls that might cause us trouble and cost money down the road, we finally come to the point where we look outside of our company, towards the partners and service providers that will help us get our plans executed.

If this is your first time trying to do transportation logistics, I'd suggest a sourcing event. Putting together all the necessary specifications, providing a deadline, and asking various carriers to quote the job. This process would vary depending on whether you're looking to complete one project or plan on working with them repeatedly over the course of business. Each one of these variables would bring different overall sourcing strategies to keep in mind.

All carriers have websites and provide literature to interested clients, so spending some time doing research, calling around, and putting together a "Top Carriers" list, could pay off down the road.

Knowing whom to call for each of your business needs streamlines your internal processes.

Once you have a list of some viable carriers that fit your transportation needs, then it's time to determine whether your needs are strategic or transactional. These two classifications bring two different methods of approaching the carrier selection process.

If this is a low-risk transactional query for a short job, a cost-focused approach makes sense. Selecting the lowest cost carrier would be your best bet. If they're not great carriers, you can discard them from your shipment pool with minimal effort and gravitate towards slightly more expensive carriers with significantly better service until you find your optimal service/cost balance.

If your needs are higher risk, then more in-depth research would be advised, particularly when it comes to their processes, reputation, and insurance requirements in case things go wrong. The more you have on the line, the more carefully you must approach each decision to safeguard your product, reputation, and business. At the end of the day, if the carrier fails to deliver your product, the customer is not going to care how much money you saved by using the cheapest carrier, but they are going to judge you harshly on your inability to meet their expectations.

If on the other hand you're looking for a long-term partner, then I'd suggest adding their customer service abilities into consideration. There's nothing more frustrating in logistics than trying to address an urgent issue and spending all day being transferred around a company's directory talking to people who can't help. There are many benefits to having a transportation partner, as it can create lots of competitive advantages and business efficiencies over companies who don't have that relationship. Creating win-win situations is crucial to building successful relationships.

Regardless of whichever situation works for your business, I recommend two business practices when dealing specifically with carriers. These practices are necessary for the continuous improvement of your company and your overall growth:

Shipment data gathering and creating carrier score cards. You don't really need any fancy resource management system to put these two suggestions in practice, but you do need a disciplined mind to implement these successfully.

Data gathering is crucial to drive continuous improvement,

because it allows for concrete data-driven decisions. In transportation. the basic measurements that you might want to keep track of for EVERY SHIPMENT, would be carrier name, time of contact, promised time of arrival, time of arrival, time of departure, time of arrival at destination, quoted cost, and invoiced cost. Using this data and some basic analytical skills, you can often deduce costs, reliability, and average times that can lead to better planning.

Once enough data is gathered, the next step would be to use that data to create carrier score cards that can be used to make faster carrier decisions for a variety of different projects. There are various methods of creating a carrier score card. A basic score card assigns scores (1 through 5 or 1 through 10) in various categories such as cost, reliability, availability, on-time delivery, customer satisfaction, ease of scheduling, size of fleet, and industry expertise.

The Best Choice

Once the best carrier for the job has been selected, it is crucial to revisit the basics to double check that nothing was missed. The best way to do this is to reiterate it in the form of clear expectations to the carrier. Remember, if a carrier agrees to do a job, it's best that you give them enough information to be able to efficiently and accurately perform it. The acronym "ASAP" might mean very different things to you and the carrier. To avoid any issues that difference might cause, I suggest putting a data package together for the carrier, to ensure that all the crucial details have been addressed in the form of a follow up email that clearly states what is expected of them, as well as points of contact they can call with any questions.

At this point, I'd like to also point out that selecting carriers you trust will go a long way, particularly when things go wrong. The expertise a carrier can bring to the table, if we can trust them to do their job well, can get you out of many difficult situations. Of course, not a single carrier will care about your business more than you will, but some carriers are without a doubt more attentive and customer focused than others.

Tracking and Tracing

Measuring progress is crucial for business processes, and there is a plethora of reasons why we need to know where our shipment is at any given moment. Depending on your business model and customer requirements, it might be necessary to put some processes in place to monitor a shipment from beginning to end. While this has a lot of benefits, it can also bring a few challenges. With big companies, there are tracking procedures for the customers that can save a lot of time. Online tracking numbers can go a long way for effective freight monitoring. With smaller companies that might not have these services, building a good relationship with the carriers can be crucial in the method of tracking and can be achieved through constant communication.

Points of Information

Every shipment will have an inherent probability that something will go wrong. When it does, it is crucial to ensure that the package and documentation gets to all the parties involve, so that effective decisions can be made as soon as possible. Depending on the company size and scope of each worker, this could be one person or several people.

The first person to call would have to be the primary decision maker for the shipment. This is the person who is responsible to ensure the shipment goes from point A to point B on behalf of the company. This is the person that needs to know if there are any delays from the plan once the shipment is on the road and the person capable of making decisions on behalf of the company. The shipment owner and the carrier company both would have their own person.

The second person to notify is the afterhours counterpart of the primary decision maker. Often we forget that when we go to sleep there is still a truck driver fueling up on caffeine with our products in tow to their destination, and when things go wrong, he needs to know who will pick up the phone when he calls.

The third contact point should be with the escalation contacts of both companies. These are the people who need to be informed when serious things happen. Managers from all parties that might need to be involved in the event of accidents, loss of property, loss of life, governmental incidents or violations.

DATA DRIVEN DECISIONS

As your company grows, everything will grow with it. The number of transactions done in a day, the value of your products, the distance your business covers, the size of the orders, and the size of the team needed to handle all of this. As the teams grow, the visibility of the decision makers shrinks. This is where data management comes into play, to provide visibility to key decision makers that may no longer be directly involved with the day to day transactions. This is a key system in building sustainable growth that is process-focused instead of people-focused.

If the company has been set up to sustain growth, one of the outputs should be a database used to make higher level decisions. Most of the time, this data can be extracted by one of many different business management systems, depending on its scope within your organization. Once this data has been extracted and cleaned, it's possible to create meaningful analyses and insights from the aggregate data.

Why is this important? More and more, companies are focusing on data driven decisions to propel the company. The same way your car communicates with you to let you know where the gas levels are, the speed in which you are driving, and the temperature, these metrics can communicate to upper management a variety of information by which they can cut costs, expand, focus on specific markets, or embark on new ventures.

Outside of data-driven decisions, good data management

practices can bring a wider array of benefits to the company, both internally and externally.

Building Trust

A key benefit of good data management is the creation of trust. As accurate data continues to pile up with a growing business, each employee can trust that the business works as it should and that everyone else is doing their part. Management can trust that their subordinates are handling critical roles in the larger scope. Employees can see where their daily job affects the grand scheme of things. Companies can ascertain whether other companies they are doing business with are living up to their contracts and promises. Over time, all of these create trust between parties as they continue to perform business with the data as accountability measurement.

Understanding the Issues
That May Arise

The next inherent benefit of good data is the visibility of issues and opportunities that each business is faced with. Data alone can't fix your business, but accurate data is the first step to actionable insights that are necessary for companies to avoid problems, find opportunities, and continue to adapt to shifting market conditions. No matter how much data you have, it will not be of any use unless you can draw meaningful insights by which to craft action plans, assign tasks, and complete projects to improve your overall key performance indicators (KPIs) and metrics.

Confidence levels

All meaningful data is drawn from non-abstract processes in real life, presenting a plethora of both known and unknown variables that could affect the numbers seen. It is crucial to understand the differences in order to discover the leverages and controls available to us. For example, a delay in shipments might be caused by bad carrier service, unrealistic lead time expectations, weather delays, or country import/export changes. Some of these are easier for us to influence than others. The main point to take away is all these meaningful insights should come with a degree of confidence as every issue can be complex beyond the initially visible or actionable.

KPIs

What each company decides to measure has mostly to do with who they are as a company, what they are trying to accomplish, and the resources available to them. Each company traditionally has sets of metrics that are tracked for general purposes by leadership. In theory, these metrics should be aligned with their business needs and goals. Oftentimes, however, they are more generic in nature and not perfectly aligned with the business. In these situations, each company is responsible for creating new metrics aligned with their company and tailoring their goals, processes, and resources to those metrics. Furthermore, crucial metrics can be turned into key performance metrics, more commonly known as Key Performance Indicators (KPI) which are used to measure the general performance of the company.

Write It Down

If you can measure it, you can control it, or so the popular theory goes. When it comes to recording data, I would highly recommend an automated process. Data entry can be a tedious and repetitive task that involves a high level of focus and accuracy from individuals. Accuracy is best left to automation; the more people involved in data entry, the less accurate the data tends to become, making it difficult to draw reliable analyses from the data. If automation is not possible, it is not an insurmountable challenge. It just needs to be a task that is addressed delicately to ensure the best results. Some of the most useful things to record would be the following, from which we can begin a cohesive process of data analysis that yields some useful insights:

1. Request entry time
2. Time actioned
3. Time to pick up
4. Time to delivery
5. Promised dates
6. Actual dates
7. Primary costs
8. Secondary or accessorial costs
9. Origin and Destinations
10. Distanced Traveled
11. People involved
12. Products moved
13. Equipment used
14. Weights and dimensions

Analyze It

The final piece of the transportation management puzzle would be to look at all the transactions done and take the data it has produced in order to optimize the entire system. Looking at the data we can extrapolate inefficiencies in our processes that might waste money. Higher level analysis can also highlight opportunities for improvements that could transform into bottom line dollars.

Asking the Right Questions

With every data analysis project, there will always be a logical starting point. The first step in successful data analysis is simply knowing what we hope to obtain from the information. Having a clearly defined goal or questions can save a lot of time and effort sorting through all the information available to you. Perhaps a good first question would be "What are we spending the most money on? And Why?" These types of questions give the data meaning. They transform all those simple data points into actionable information that can drive our business decisions.

Other useful questions for data analysis would be:

1. Where is the biggest consolidation of activity?
2. Are there any patterns between two parameters?
3. Where is most of our profits coming from?
4. Who is responsible for the most common outliers?
5. Are there any visible areas of improvement?
6. Who are we spending the most money on?
7. Who are we doing the most transactions with?
8. Who is charging the most per transaction?
9. Are there any known reasons for the current state of business reflected in the data?
10. Where do we see the most opportunity to save money?

Cutting up the data

Once we have some answers extrapolated from the data, the next step would be to "slice and dice" the data. This is the process in which we gather, standardize, classify, and analyze all the data available and turn it into actionable insights. This can come in many forms and use a variety of different software. The current industry standard and the most widely available form of data analysis software is using Microsoft Excel. It is extremely versatile, readily available, and commonly known. However, for stronger data analysis needs, there is more capable software such as Tableau, Qlikview, or Power BI that provide further insights.

When cutting up the data there are a few guidelines that make the whole project more profitable for everyone:

1. Look at the information from as many different points of view as possible (accounting, operations, management, and product line)
2. Look at the information through various parameters (time, category, products, product families, cost, and volume)
3. Look at the information represented in as many views (bar charts, pie charts, pivot tables, scatter charts, area charts, and Pareto charts)
4. Bring subject matter experts (SMEs) in to interpret the information (sometimes the best point of views come from multiple people looking at the data.)
5. Always ask WHY?

BEST PRACTICES

As an ending to this book, I decided to go over a few good practices and ideas that make logistics a little bit less stressful for all players involved. These are a few simple suggestions that can go a long way towards minimizing issues and maximizing efficiencies.

Using Data Packages

Using "data packages" or complete sets of information when communicating about a product or shipment helps ensure that everyone involved is on the same page. I can't tell you how often I've seen emails with one reference number that connects to a system that not everyone is able to access. Angry emails from one of the thousands of employees at my company complaining that the truck they requested never arrived, without a single reference to which of the hundreds of shipments we've recently handled they're referring to. Trucking requests from a requestor that mysteriously disappears when we're asking for clarification necessary to move the products. For these and many other reasons, it is always a good practice to use complete data packages that can be passed around to all involved parties.

If this is not possible, the next best option is to always take the extra few seconds needed to be extra thorough when communicating about products, shipments, or movements.

This means, using multiple reference identifiers, adding easily recognizable data bits, and coherent information.

For example:

"Subject: 876357293 Email: Please advise status" has a lot more risk of being misunderstood or simply ignored than something along the lines of "Subject: Shipment 876357293 Houston, Texas, to Oklahoma City, Oklahoma. Email: John, Please advise the current status of Shipment 876357293. It was picked up at the Houston location yesterday morning, and the crew in Oklahoma City would like to know when it's estimated to arrive so they can plan accordingly. Oklahoma crew in copy."

Planning Ahead

Planning in logistics may seem like a logical step, but most of the opportunities and cost savings can be realized the longer the planning horizon becomes. This allows time for alternatives, negotiations, and consolidations significantly reducing total transportation costs. The more urgent the request, the highest the overall costs are in general.

Planning can also lead to less stress for the people moving these shipments, leading to a more positive work environment. These planning horizons alone, however, are not enough to save the company millions of dollars, particularly when there are other factors influencing the transportation spend, such as contracts in place, rigid processes, methodologies, or seller's markets.

Resource Utilization

If you're already paying for something, make sure you take full advantage of it. Whether it's filling up the space in the dedicated trucks you source or fully utilizing all the features in the new software you're installing. Everything you neglect to use is money that could have been better used elsewhere.

I've seen multiple examples in multiple companies of departments with multiple software implemented that have related or similar functionality that is currently being underutilized, instead of having a few systems that are completely and thoughtfully integrated. Even worse, I've seen cases where the systems are disconnected, and the only connections between systems are the people that have to take all the information from one system and try to recreate a big portion of it on a different system.

Keep on Reading On...

As the last piece of advice, I know one thing to be true in this world, and it's that the world will continue to change. So, I urge each person reading this book to make an active effort to continue to read, learn, and move forward.

Thank you for reading.

THE TRANSPORTATION REQUEST CHECKLIST

Considerations
1. Is it physically possible to do?
2. Is it legal to do?
3. Can I afford to do it?
4. What all can stop me, or slow me down while I'm doing it?

Necessary Information
1. Origin
   a. Address
   b. Contact person
   c. Contact Phone
   d. Operating Hours
2. Destination
   a. Address
   b. Contact person
   c. Contact Phone
   d. Operating Hours
3. Dates and Times
   a. Pick up time
   b. Delivery Time
4. Equipment Required
5. Cargo

      a. Units
      b. Packaging
      c. Dimensions
      d. Weight
      e. Description
      f. Hazmat
      g. Reference Numbers
      h. Totals

6. Notes

APPENDIX

LOGISTICS AXIOMS

1. Murphy's law, everything that can go wrong, will go wrong, so be aware and ready.

2. What you don't know, can hurt you, so spend time daily bettering yourself, reading, running through scenarios, perfecting your processes etc.

3. Everybody sees the world different, the word "fast" to you might mean something different to your employees, to your coworkers, to your teammates, to your customers, so always be as specific and clear as possible.

CARGO
CONSIDERATIONS

- How much space do I need?
- How much weight do I need to consider?
- What is the best mode of transport?
- What precautions do I need to take for the safe transport of the product?
- What precautions do I need to take for the safety of all those involved in the movement?
- What legal and financial guidelines apply?
- What challenges am I going to find while trying to move this?
- Is this a strategic move, or a transactional move?
- What loading and offloading requirements does this face?
- Are the dimensions correct?
- What equipment is necessary to move this?
- Is this material stackable or not?
- Will I need any oversized permits?
- Can this go in a smaller vehicle with acceptable overhang?
- Will the dimensions affect my trucking options?